I Just Bought
My Elephant

I Just Bought
My Elephant

Be Stubborn, Get Rich and Prosper

Nantu Majumdar

PARTRIDGE
A Penguin Random House Company

To order additional copies of this book, contact
Partridge India
000 800 10062 62
orders.india@partridgepublishing.com

www.partridgepublishing.com/india

Contents

Acknowledgement

I want to thank my family for being my motivation, my strength and my inspiration in life that makes me chase my dreams with confidence.

Introduction

As a boy, I grew up in a not so rich locality and have seen my parents "struggle", as much as I saw others in my neighborhood. "Struggle" to win some race, a race that kept them busy from morning to evening. They dealt with so many complications and went through so much stress. They had their moments of joy but they were few and far in between. This "Struggle" was to realize their dream of being prosperous, for the sake of their own and for their children's sake. So they woke up early morning to begin "the struggle". The struggle to reach office on time, the struggle to achieve the sales targets, the struggle to be the better employee for that lucrative promotion, the struggle to complete a report before a deadline or the struggle to complete the preparation for audits, to meet the deadline on filing of taxes, to make the children merit holders in class, to make more money month on month and year on year and so on. We do it and in all probability, our parents and elders also did it before us, but nobody seems to be enjoying it, while they still lived day in and out in the "struggle".

The retired often got together and spoke how difficult it is to live a retired life, and how they were making compromises to meet their family requirements. Again, nobody was really happy. I always wondered why? Surprisingly, I saw concern amongst the rich as well; prime amongst them was fear of losing everything, dysfunctional relationships, radically changing family values, sibling rivalry on inheritance and more. Even with increasing wealth and professional growth there existed a huge gap in their minds that never seem to fill so the effort and the rush to fill it never quite finished. So, less money is a problem but the answer does not seem to be in simply having more money. But then, how much money is enough money? Is there a limit or a figure, which once earned will bring financial stability and we will be out of this "Struggle? Or was there any particular thing or standard that once achieved satisfied our drive to attain prosperity, and we could say that we are now prosperous... I don't think so.

What does this "Prosperity" mean to us? Frankly speaking initially to me, and I am sure to most of us, it meant having more money. It was the spending power of money that could buy me my dream house, my dream car, my vacation at the best of locations, providing the best of facilities to my family and for myself as well. Nothing wrong

Contrary to my belief that this was all about money, this travel took me through the lanes and by lanes of my strongest beliefs and my personality traits and put to test the thoughts and values I so dearly held on to.

with that, after all we all want to prosper. If I went by that understanding then why were some of the rich not so prosperous, why do some rich become poor, non-prosperous? Many of the rich did not get richer, and not all of them were happy. Something was missing here, and the missing piece was happiness. Having the wealth was important, but along with it was important to be happy and satisfied as well.

I spent the first 6 years of my professional life as an infantry officer with the Indian Army. I almost never focused on wealth or prosperity. I earned and spent money when I could and did it so well. The army takes good care of you so my cost of living and that of my family was a given, never a challenge. I never had to be concerned about it. I was only 24 years when I enlisted with the army, then came marriage and then children my life had started changing. After I completed my tenure with the army, I joined the corporate world and began the cycle of waiting for pay cheques. Strangely, the money that got credited in my account would diminish faster than I expected or planned for and all that we managed doing is meeting the daily and monthly expense. I had already compromised on the standard of living. Then I also had to worry about my children's future and high cost of education. I am sure you may have experienced or seen others go through such experiences. I too had started living the "Struggle" and at time felt my life was falling apart, It was at this time that I decided to turn things around for myself and for my family. I read about successful people and their path to success, interacted with those who were financially independent some of whom are very dear friends, I also studied the unsuccessful and learning from each one of them and thanks to this learning I was able to fairly chalk out a road map to "Prosperity", but the learnings continued with every step.

Having a fairly sketchy idea as to why the Rich only Prosper while the others continue the "struggle", I took off on the path to Prosperity. Contrary to my belief that this was all about money, this travel took me through the lanes and by lanes of my strongest beliefs and my personality traits and put to test the thoughts and values I so dearly held on to.

Through this book, I am attempting to share my learning of this journey that I acquired through my experiences and that of the experiences of the other that I saw.

My Elephant

In India, we tell a lot of stories, stories that pass on our values and culture through the generations. My mother has been one of the greatest story tellers that I have come across in my lifetime. As a child I listened to her for hours and lived the epic wars, humor and the mythology that she told me as I passed into my dreams every night. Two animals in particular had a significant impact on me, the first one is the Horse and the second is the Elephant. While the horse represented speed, action and thrill, the Elephant meant Royalty, Prosperity, Power, longevity and Stability.

In India, the elephant is found in the form of Lord Ganesha who is the god of luck, fortune and protection. He is worshiped before any other God. Lord Ganesha in all his vibrant glory and grace defeats all obstacles for all his worshipers and blesses them with Prosperity. Other cultures also symbolize the elephant with happiness, longevity and good luck.

In Chinese art, the elephant is a symbol of wisdom and strength. Elephant is also considered a sacred animal in Buddhist traditions. Buddha is often depicted riding an elephant. These magnificent creatures are also regarded as auspicious figures in Thailand. Elephants have a reputation in both Indian and Chinese culture for attracting wealth and good luck.

Only the Kings, the Royals ever owned Elephants in the stories that I heard. They were superior, rich and prosperous; they had the best of everything and always lived in abundance. I romanced the idea of living in abundance at that early age. To improve my standard of living to that of a Royal, or in the modern world, like the Rich and Prosperous, I had to build capabilities to buy my Elephant.

The Elephant to me is the epitome of "Prosperity".

Getting Started By defining Success

Defining Success is important. While you would want to Prosper, when would you know that you have prospered and are now Rich or Wealthy? I was clear right from the start (so I thought) that I want to be more Richer than Mr abc/- in my locality, who has a lavish lifestyle. He owned an expensive car and can afford foreign vacations every year, his children went to an expensive school and they always were on top of fashion. My understanding crashed like a pack of cards the day their expensive car was towed away by the mortgage company from just outside our residential compound. They suddenly they did not look very Rich and Prosperous to me. They had the lifestyle, they were surrounded by luxury but they were really not prosperous. So my definition of Rich possessing all these luxury materials around them was surely not correct.

My next idol of Rich was my aunt. She had acquired a large inheritance and had loads of money in her bank account and earned a bank interest that she happily spent, some were stacked away in fixed deposits. Everything was fine, till the government decided to drop interest rates and increased Income Tax, the spending went down and at one point in time she took up a part time job as well. So my definition of Rich having a lot of money also faded away.

Lost for definition, I kept my search on. If having the luxury that the Rich can afford and having lots of money was not the answer then what was?

My understanding that having a luxurious life style meant that you were RICH faded away.

Most of the unsuccessful people I studied, defined success differently than those who were successful. The difference was not making "Money" but the way they spent it. Money was the scale used as a measure by both, one was short term and the other was long term. The unsuccessful worked to earn "Lots of Money". Having lot of money to them meant that they had the means to be wealthy and all their current challenges would be met and their future would be secure. Yet they would find it difficult to recall where the last bonus money they received went. The salaries received in the beginning of the month vanished much before the end of the month. They completed the month with little and no surplus to invest. The

While the unsuccessful thought of spending, the successful were thinking of earning more. This difference originates from completely divergent Beliefs and thought process, eventually leading to different actions and different results.

new month only saw the cycle repeat itself. The successful, on the other hand defined it more in terms of the ability of keep generating more money. Their focus was also generating more money in the long run but the immediate focus was to keep on increasing their avenues to make more money. This was the fundamental difference, while the unsuccessful thought of spending, the successful were thinking of earning more. This difference originates from completely divergent Beliefs and thought process, eventually leading to different actions and different results.

For a brief period in my career, I was assigned project that required me to drive down over 95 km to work daily and back, I am sure that this is a big deal in most part of the world, in India this surely was. The assignment was critical and as a loyal employee and an ex-army man there was no way I was backing out. So I picked up my SUV and travelled the paths less travelled by me earlier. The drive was a pleasurable one especially in the wee hours of the morning. I was often tempted to make a halt at a small tea stall en route. It was under a huge banyan tree that afforded a lot of shade. Sipping tea under the tree with the fragrance of the country side was a wonderful feeling. Many of my fellow travelers would stop by. The tea stall was busy all the time with some really varied expensive cars parked out most of the time that I remember. I could not help but notice a branded coffee wending machine. The owner was courteous and simple. I asked him why he kept the coffee wending machine here. He said the company sales rep had told him that it would attract more people and that many people prefer having coffee from this company, besides he pays me Rs2000/- per month to keep the machine and for every cup of coffee I get 50 paisa for it, so I let it be, but my tea sell more than the coffee, he laughed. I thanked him for the special tea paid him continued my journey to my workplace.

After a tiring day, on my way back I glanced at the tea shop and the words of the owner flashed back in my mind. Suddenly I realized that something very unique had happened. I parked by the road side amazed at what I had realized. My mind was stuck on a flicker of a thought. Here was a man involved in his daily business to earn his monies. By allowing the coffee wending machine he had managed to assure himself a fixed income and an incremental income which did not involve him. In addition, he never had to spend any effort to earn it. The only time he got involved, is during the month end to collect the money. If the machine was not operational he would intimate the engineer who would come and repair it. For the time the machine would not be operational, his incremental revenue would be hit not his fixed income. With this money he could pay off his liabilities that he would otherwise be paid out of his earnings from the tea stall thus making his income swell. It was another matter that the tea stall owner did not see what I saw, I studied him better in the next few days to understand his spending habit. This is a subject of another discussion.

I realized that while I was making money in my current job, it was my current liabilities that were eating into it and reducing my income, leaving very little to invest or spend leading me to remain in my "Struggle". So what I needed to have is ancillary fixed income and incremental income which did not require my involvement or a minimum involvement. This will help me in building my surplus funds on a continuous basis. When I have surplus funds, I can have the luxury items without the fear of losing them to mortgage and the loads of money in my bank without the government derailing my plans. While they would add to my income my dependence on them would not be absolute as I still have my daytime job.

So with this new learning, I decided to define the financial part of being Prosperous as ***"generating ancillary fixed income and incremental income twice my monthly liability".*** The reasoning behind twice was that for every month of ancillary income generated I would cover the liabilities of 2 months, thus making the second month income free of liabilities. In the second month the ancillary incomes adds to my surplus or can be used to cover the liabilities of the next two months. Also, being a target driven person, it was important I set myself a challenging goal. Even if I reached half I would still win, now that is not what I was thinking I was targeting 100%.

Simple I said to myself, but when I looked at where I can start, I drew a blank. I am sure you would feel the same. But hey we are just getting started.

Building a "Resilient" Self

Resilience is adapting well in the face of adversity. It means "bouncing back" from difficult experiences, dealing with things that stress you out, put you down and hold you back from chasing that BIG dream that is so important to you. Being resilient does not mean that we become immune to stress, or that the difficulties vanishes, it actually prepares to you deal with it and yet achieve your dream. It involves beliefs, behaviors and thoughts that can be learned and developed by anyone. Being resilient is important for us to achieve our Dream of Prosperity. This would mean that we question and relook at our beliefs, thoughts and actions. Build the capacity to make realistic plans and take steps to carry them out. Build confidence in one's own self and in our strengths and abilities. Look to solve problems and build the capacity to manage strong feelings, impulses and deal with demotivating influences.

"Stubborn Positivity"

In my army tenure, after I completed my training, I joined my battalion when they were posted eye ball to eye ball with the enemy on a treacherous mountainous terrain, I experienced many life changing experiences while in the army. These have been my teachers and the lessons learnt can possibly never been forgotten. Like the very first encounter with death; which I survived to tell the tale. No it was not a heroic assault on the enemy post or anything of that sort; it was peace times after all. As a young newly commissioned infantry officer, I was going to take over the charge of my own post. The journey included a 3 hour of climb at an average height of 17500ft. The air is thinner and the oxygen levels are low. At these heights, the melting snow creates multiple streams that usually make very fast flowing rivers that are not very broad but deep. The water falling from these heights create beautiful waterfalls but are very rough and dangerous. In the month of Dec, the snow peaks. At these heights, 'single man track' is used to move from one post to another. As we repeatedly walk this beaten track, the snow on the track solidifies. Moving towards my post, my first independent command, to live all that I had dreamt as a boy, I was in a hurry. 4 Soldiers and I armed with light weapons began the scale upwards on a narrow, single man track. The Himalayas are treacherous but beautiful. The foot track we were on had many steep fall and steep climbs from time to time. As we climbed along a deep valley the weather changed suddenly and the entire valley was engulfed in a snow storm. Helplessly we watched the forces of nature engulf us. The resultant "whiteout" situation was bad and visibility dropped to near zero. Undaunted, we inched forward. After almost 2 hours we reached flat ground. My initial reaction was that it was the post, but no it was not. The snow was beating our faces continuously, the visibility continued to be nearly zero, and we lost our track. We looked around desperately, moved a few feet around to try and find our track again, but we did not find it.

My life changed that moment. I was in trouble, but all that I could see was the soldiers they were looking up to me for my reaction. Without showing my own fear I started focusing on them, to get them to safety and back to the post.

Right from the start of the climb we were edging along the sides of the waterfall. The fall was ferocious was about a 1000 feet or so. As we were looking for our foot track the sound of the water grew louder and louder. As we continued our search, suddenly we began slipping. I touched the ground only to realize we were standing on ice, directly over the waterfall, with the river water viciously flowing below us. To what I know the ice would be very thin in this area. If the ice cracked, we would be swept with the water straight a 1000, feet below. The realization that this could be the end sent a chill down my spine. This was not the way I had planned to die; it had to be glorious death not just an accident.

My life changed that moment. I was in trouble, but all that I could see was the soldiers they were looking up to me for my reaction. Without showing my own fear I stated focusing on them, to get them to safety and back to the post. An inner force that was stubborn and made me only think positive engulfed me, and I led the fight back to reverse the situation. I was acknowledging all the risks as I lead the team but my mind stubbornly stayed focused on the desired result. Leading the way ahead we inched back to our track slowly and surely and away from the waterfall. There were times where the snow level crossed our shoulders. Keeping the team together, acting decisively and keeping the morale of my team high and not allowing them to focus on fear, as a team we made it and celebrated when we reached the post. I termed that state of mind as "Stubborn Positivity".

"Stubborn Positivity" is actually a way of life. It is a culmination of your efforts to actualize your dreams with all your enthusiasm, determination that is soaked in faith and belief. It is a state of mind that acknowledges the existence of risks and hurdles, it challenges and defies them. It is a state of mind that brings you to a supreme state where your mind seeks and finds solutions and stubbornly resists attempts to demoralize and destabilize. In such a state of mind you will always have a smile in your mind and heart, no matter what situation you are in. You attract and acquire a lot of positive feeling in this state.

If this sounds complicated then make a small start. The next time a situation makes your forehead frown, make a conscious effort to remove the frown immediately, SIMPLY REMOVE THE CURVES ON YOUR FOREHEAD and you will start to feel the positive energy. This could be the start of "Stubborn Positivity" for you.

<u>Being "Stubborn Positivity" is the first attitude that you need to acquire to make this transition to being Rich and Prosperous.</u>

Our Belief Systems

Our Belief Systems are an important part of our existence. What we believe motivates and inspires us every day. It is a driving force that enables us to take actions to achieve our dreams and take risk as well. It is belief that is a deciding factor in our decision making when we evaluate risk to reward feasibility of something that we are going to do. Belief is an assumption that something exists or is true although you may not have a definite proof of it, it is an assumption of an event occurring although there may be multiple variables influencing the occurrence of that event.

Beliefs are important because they regulate our thinking, which in turn regulates our behavior and actions. Our behavior and actions has implications and results in certain outcomes, these outcomes either reinforce our beliefs or make us disbelieve. So if I wake up one day and am generally not feeling great and I believe that today's day will not go well and if I miss my regular train to office, I reinforce the belief that today's day will be bad. Amazingly though, if I manage to board the same train I necessarily need not believe that today will be a good day.

Our experiences have a profound impact on our beliefs. No matter what we believe in, there can be no substitute to what we understand from experience. So our experience says that the sun rises every morning, hence we believe that it will rise tomorrow as well. The fact is, if the planetary alignments remain the same as yesterday, the sun will rise or we could experience something different altogether, this possibility exists. It is our day to day experience starting right from our childhood days from the time when we were aware of our conscious self, we have experienced, experienced situations, events and reacted and believed and grown. Our beliefs are deep routed in these experiences.

For our beliefs to change we have to have different experience, different experience comes from experiencing different results which are an outcome of different behavior, which in turn comes from a different Belief. Now, this is easier said than done, we all know that, but the fact is that my existing beliefs and behavior have kept me from being Prosperous, which is my desired result.

Being Prosperous or not is actually a state of your mind that is engrained in beliefs. The key to making a transition from being Non Prosperous to Prosperous is to change your belief systems. Consider this,

Wealthy make their Resources work hard for their money, others work hard themselves for their money. Wealthy spend to build new opportunities that grow cash flow, others spend more on "Wants" that reduce cash

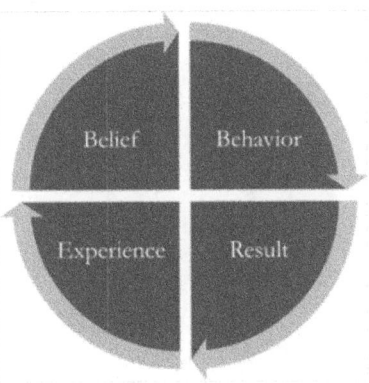

flow. Wealthy look for opportunity in change, others gets threatened by change. Wealthy concentrates on making more money, others concentrate on not losing money. Wealthy work to make profits, others work to earn more and more money. Wealthy look to convert opportunities and make money, others find obstacles in opportunities. Wealthy look to pay themselves from the results they deliver, others want to get paid for the time that they spend working. The belief systems are very different. Since the beliefs are different, the behavior is different, since the behavior is different, the results are different, since the results are different the experiences are different, which I turn confirms the Beliefs.

In this journey to get Prosperous is it important that we question our existing beliefs, revalidate them and if need be change them. We may not at this point in time have the experience to confirm our new beliefs, so let us learn from the experiences of others.

Emotional Currency

Understanding emotions is complicated, especially human emotion. From not so trivial matters like the sudden burst of emotions while driving, when overtaken wrongly and dangerously or the dislike towards your neighbor who has kept the music loud which ruined your peaceful Sunday afternoon to more serious matters. Like the story of a mother whose son was in a Juvenile prison. I was in my first job at the time, after my army tenure. As part of the company's Corporate Social Responsibility program we had tied up with an NGO involved in the rehabilitation of young children below the age of 18 years serving prison terms in a juvenile prison for some very serious crimes. It was my 4th day at the rehabilitation center and I was quite enjoying it. The youngest child was about 7 years old and the oldest would not be more than 15 for sure. This 7 year old was the naughtiest of them all and the most spirited. He was the darling of most of the volunteers there. His mother would cook his meals from home and feed him every day. She would talk and talk and caress her child and weep and weep. The boy would console her and promise her to be a good boy and take care of her when he comes back to her. Once lunch time was over, she would gather all her strength and leave her child behind while the boy would cry out to his mother as she left. The boy would be depressed for a long time and take his time to come to terms with the reality of his life pick himself up and move on. This he did every day of the days that he had spent in the juvenile prison. This young boy was serving a sentence for murder that he committed during an attempted robbery. Some of the women volunteers of the NGO had befriended his mother and were helping her develop tailoring skills for her to be able to be self-reliant.

The volunteers would spend a few moments consoling her and she would cry keep repeating that "I know my son he cannot kill anybody". The whole incident had a deep impact on me, how even a mother cannot be correct about her own child. If a mother cannot be correct about her own child, then no one possibly can.

Emotion is a complex state of feeling that influence thought and behavior. It influences changes in our psychological state influencing temperament, personality, mood and motivation. The unpredictability of emotion of an individual in a given situation makes it a dangerous and a potent force that can make the individual do wonders much beyond his own belief both constructively or destructively, most importantly, it can be contagious.

As an infantry officer, we have courses for specialized operations that we need to attend and qualify. Most of these courses are conducted in inhospitable terrain and the training standards are very high. In one such course, we had officers from friendly countries doing the course with us. The rugged terrain and temperatures touching 47 degree centigrade proved too much for one of the officers from the friendly country contingent. The first few days were very taxing on him, personally I thought he might choose to exit the course. The long cross country military training exercises across treacherous mountainous terrain was a killer especially for someone with a steel rod in his left foot. The officer had his left foot shattered in combat and the bone was replaced with a steel rod. In the very first major training exercise he was brought to the medical team, dehydrated, and semi-conscious. Emotionally shattered, his pride and ego of a Special Forces officer bruised very badly, but he was not amongst those who could be written off. This solider fought back in the balance days of the course. He not only finished the course successfully, he also won the "Best in Physicals" award.

Emotions are double edged weapons. We can either let it work upon us and destroy us or we can choose to use it to get where we want to and achieve what we want to. The question is how we are choosing to use our emotions. Tough as it may sound but it is still a choice.

> Emotions are double edged weapons. We can either let it work upon us and destroy us or we can choose to use it to get where we want to and achieve what we want to. The question is how we are choosing to use our emotions

In our relentless drive to "Prosper", we, on a continuous basis, look to achieve so many milestones that we set for ourselves. We chase our dreams with enthusiasm, passion and give it our complete best. We battle, we manage, and we negotiate through all the hurdles and obstacles that come our way. We sometimes win and sometimes we do not. Regardless of the outcome of the milestones we are chasing, we have a high degree of emotional involvement. When we succeed we feel energized, have a sense of achievement and it motivates us to achieve higher goals and reach the next milestone. However the reverse happens when we do not win, we feel frustrated and demotivated. In both the cases I am a spending what I call my "emotional Currency". So when I win I get my "Return on Investment (ROI)" and when I do not succeed I lose my investment. Higher the emotional involvement greater in the emotional currency I am spending. This is a limited supply currency. Just as when I purchase an item and pay money for it I expect the best quality and will want to enjoy the benefits of the item that I am buying. Similarly, when I am spending my emotional currency to actualize my dream or my milestone, I look to achieve and win. If I spend my emotional

This implies that we must be very selective on the battles we choose to fight and fight we must, to win. You cannot fight all battles and win them all. While losing a few battles is ok it is important to win the war, which is your dream of "Prosperity".

currency on too many dreams and too many milestones, with my limited supply of Emotional Currency I may not be able to passionately drive to achieve my milestones to "Prosperity", so the chances of failure increase. This implies that we must be very selective on the battles we choose to fight and fight we must, to win. You cannot fight all battles and win them all. While losing a few battles is ok it is important to win the war, which is your dream of "Prosperity".

The Mathematics problem

Mathematics was never my favorite subject while at school. I always had to put in additional efforts to score well, something that came quite naturally to a few others in my class. Being a "Not So Bright" student in the class I always found myself spending quite a few weekends attending extra class. The extra practice in my coaching class was also no fun. Problems like, Jack was travelling from city 'A' to city 'B' that was "___ Miles" away he was driving in his old car that gave him a milage of "___ Km" to a liter of petrol, his car had a capacity to hold "__ gallons" of fuel and had a dimension of "L*B*H". The tank had a hole of measuring "—"in diameter. So how much time will he take to reach city 'B' and what will be his fuel consumption. My child's mind would always question "Why the hell Jack went to city 'B'? If at all he had to go he could have taken the subway or a Bus? While my mind kept on with

At school we always got marks to solve the Math problem and not crib over it. Even in real live we benefit by solving them. We had limited time then so is the case with real life problems.

these thoughts, others quickly got on to solving the problem. The typical approach was to note down the facts of the problems and then start the process of solving them and they would finish solving them on time and get the marks. The fact of the case was that, even if "Jack" was not travelling, probably "Jill" would have or may be "Mary" how does it matter who was travelling in the problem. The reality was that there was a problem and that it had to be solved. We got our marks for that and we had to operate in the limited time frame that we had.

This thought and realization stayed with me much beyond my student years. It helped me resolve a lot of conflicts with others as well as within myself as well. The technique is very simple and the younger you are (at heart that is) the easier it is to implement. My 7 year old daughter one evening had a disagreement with my wife. The topic was the pretty big for her, but for us it was a parenting issue that we had to handle carefully. She had recently enrolled into a specialized coaching class that would give her a sound foundation in critical subjects like mathematics and science. As part of the curriculum, the children had to complete an assignment and had 4 days to do so. She has morning school from 7am to 2pm and during the week she has her "Karate" class twice a week, "Singing" class once a week. School homework takes on an average 2 hours to complete and she plays with her friends for about 3 hours daily, oh and I forgot to mention, she sleeps in the afternoon after lunch for 2-3 hours. The assignment was expected to take 2 hours a day (approximately, and completely depended on how much time she could sit at one place without being distracted) if she had to complete it in 4 days. (This sounds like my math problem I was talking about). With the assignment getting added on, she would have no time to play. Both sides stood their ground and were not willing to compromise. Just as my daughter reached a dead end in the discussion with my wife, she unleashed the ultimate weapon, the little girl was all in tears. So she came to me with her sobs powering her emotional plea that could have melted a rock, I was only a human and her father too. How many times and in so many ways we realize Parenting is not easy. Resisting the great urge to succumb to her tears and giving in to her demands, I decided to give my technique a try.

Every problem typically comes attached with emotions; it could be anger, hate and sometimes even optimism. It is important to defuse this inflated emotional balloon. With emotions dominating your thinking, no rational decision can ever be taken. So I put my listening skills to good use as she detailed out her dilemma to me as she let her precious tears flow by. I paid full attention to her and disallowed any distractions. I cross checked and confirmed that I understood her well, and in due process exposed her just a little bit to a few options to her dilemma, soon the monolog turned to dialogue and the emotions were drained out. Now she was ready to get... let say "Mathematical". I told her that there was actually no problem at all, it was simple math. She looked surprised, what has math got to do with it? I asked her to grab a paper and pencil which she did.

I asked her to list out all that she does in a day and the hours that it takes. She wrote,

1. School hours – 6 Hours
2. Lunch and afternoon Sleep – 2 Hours
3. Homework – 1 Hour
4. Play time – 2 Hours
5. Classes (Singing and Karate) – 2 Hours
6. Dinner and Night sleep & ready for school – 9 Hours

Great I said, I then asked her to total the number of hours; correctly so she said 22 Hours she suddenly realized that she had 2 hours extra that she generally spent without a great sense of purpose. Having driven the possibility with her I helped her detail it.

Activity	Hours	Time from	Time to
School Hours	6	07:00 AM	13:00 PM
Lunch and afternoon sleep	2	13:00 PM	15:00 PM
Homework	1	15:00 PM	16:00 PM
Play	2	16:00 PM	18:00 PM
Classes (Singing / Karate)	2	18:00 PM	20:00 PM
Available Hours	2	20:00 PM	22:00 PM
Dinner and Night sleep & ready for school	9	22:00 PM	07:00 AM
Total Hours	24		

Suddenly she believed that she could get to play and complete the assignment, a complete win-win she grabbed it. Armed with a solution, she decided to reinitiate the discussion with my wife who was in the kitchen giving the finishing touches to some yummy dinner. Mom, she said, ok I will do the assignment as you want it, but you must buy me my favorite chocolate in return. My wife quickly agreed and added only after you finish the assignment, she was pleased with the change. Now, where did my daughter learn to negotiate like that? You know, another thing about Parenting is that at every stage you realize that your child has grown a little more and generally does not fail to surprise you.

This example may be oversimplified, not all situations can be listed out in numbers as I did in the example above, but the approach has always worked, what often is the challenge is the will to implement the solution.

The Game of Chess

My son was introduced to the game of Chess pretty early in his childhood. My wife thought it was a good idea to encourage him to learn the game as it "Exercises the mind" and I agreed. So we enrolled him under a reputed instructor and his training began. He learnt fast and was enjoying it. He would look forward to the class and had made a friend with some of the good students. While my wife would regularly drop him to the class and pick him up after the class my role was limited. After almost two weeks of him starting the chess coaching, I had an opportunity to pick him up from class as my wife had prior engagements. So there I was standing at the gates waiting for my bright star to come running to me as he would not be expecting me there. Well he was excited at first and then, "where is mom?" he handed me the bag and continued speaking to his friend. They were deep into a discussion on a game, what I heard stunned me for a while,

My son: Pawn to e4

His friend: Pawn to e6

My son: Pawn to d4

His friend: Pawn to d5

My son: Pawn to e5

His friend: Pawn to c5

My son: Pawn to c3

His friend: Queen to b6

My son: Pawn to b3

His friend: Knight to e7

My son: Bishop to e3

His friend: Knight from b8 to c6

The last I knew, my son could speak English, what language or dialect was this. Just then I realized... they were playing a game of chess ... verbally, in their mind. God my heart skipped a beat, but I was proud of him and respected his involvement in the game.

He was doing well at the game and the coach was happy with his progress. He was of the opinion that my son should participate in the upcoming city level tournaments that will give him an opportunity to play with experienced participants and aid his learning, I agreed.

It was a bright Sunday morning and many children had turned out for the tournament that day. Many were nervous while still many more were pretty confident calm and composed. My little fella was calm but there was a storm inside. This was his first tournament, and it was a huge one for his little baby steps, he was just 8 years then.

My wife and I used all our counselling skills to calm him and help him to do his very best. The first round began, and our wait started. 30 minutes into the game we saw few children coming out of the competition area, as our eyes were glues to the entrance to the competition area. Just as I thought that my little fella would be engaged in a good battle, given that he spent so much time in there I saw his feet drag his crouched body that suspended his little head like a walking lamp post. I knew the result immediately and also that I need to hold and support my little boy right away. The defeat had shattered his ego and pride. My wife immediately went into analysis mode after pacifying him and corrected the mistakes that he did. I could clearly see that this was not doing any good to his current emotional state. I had a few words of encouragement as well before he went to his next round. They were playing to the best of 10. This time he came out after 1 hour 45 minutes, my wife and I looked at him as he came out of the entrance to the competition area. This time he was angry as well, we instantly knew that he had lost the game. Angrily he told my wife, he was winning and then he did a silly mistake and lost the game. His opponent was a senior player, he came looking for my son and told him that he had played fantastically. He told me that initially my son was losing and then he fought back and came to a winning position. His morale boosted and in the excitement he threw caution to the air and the result was that he lost from a winning position. Complemented by the opponent made my son feel better and the anger was gone. During the lunch break I stole some time to speak to him. Trying to connect to the game of chess I thought it was time to have a father to son chat.

Sipping a soft drink we sat on a stone bench just outside the premises. It was noisy, but that was the best that we could have got. I told him how proud he made us by the efforts he was putting in. But baba (father), he said, I did not win my game, I am not just good enough. True I said, you are not actually, he was surprised, he was not expecting that. I carried on, from a technical point you are good, your opponent actually walked up to you and said so, so technically you are good. It is your mental makeup that is the problem. He had a confused look, exactly

Battles are won and lost in your mind first then on ground and history is evidence to this. So the question comes down to what are you thinking about, "Joy of winning" or the "Fear of losing"?

what I was hoping for; he was now going to listen.

When the chess board was prepared at the start of the game did any of the player have an advantage, he said no, did any of the blacks or whites not in their right place when they started, they were in the right place he said, the pawn, the rook the minister all followed what you asked them to do, did any of them disobey you, he said surely not, how can they. Then my son the way I look at it is that you lost the game in your mind and it started at the time of starting the game. Fear of losing guided you rather than the joy of winning, so you lost. Play for the joy of winning and the chances are that you will win. Battles are won and lost in your mind first then on ground and history is evidence to this. So the question comes down to what are you thinking about, "Joy of winning" or the "Fear of losing"?

I asked him what happened in the last game, your opponent said you were in a losing position, "yes" he acknowledged. From a losing position straight to a winning position, how could you manage? "I had lost the previous game so I kept on telling myself that I had to win, I had to win". So, I said, "that motivated you to do well. When you started doing well, you got into a pseudo feeling that you are winning and that you will make it this time and the previous loss will be wiped out", "yes" he said. So besides the "Fear of losing" driving your thoughts and actions; there is one more thing that I want you to know, his eyes grew in expectation. After you have played the game what happens to the chess pieces? Promptly he said we rearrange the board before we leave the table. Great I said, so the previous position has no bearing on the very next game, "No" he said, regardless of you winning it or your opponent winning it. So all the pieces go back from their respective position from where they have won or lost to start afresh. Son, take the experience to the next game but not the emotions attached either to winning or losing, the results of the previous game has no bearing on the outcome of the next. The next game is a fresh one. He nodded in acknowledgement. You know, we adults find it very difficult to do this in our lives, but if

When the chess board was prepared at the start of the game did any of the player have an advantage, he said no, did any of the blacks or whites not in their right place when they started, they were in the right place he said, the pawn, the rook the minister all followed what you asked them to do, did any of them disobey you, he said surely not, how can they. Then my son the way I look at it is that you lost the game in your mind and it started at the time of starting the game. Fear of losing guided you rather than the joy of winning.

you can do it now you will be far more successful than what you would otherwise be. He stayed fixed on me as I spoke, absorbing everything what I was telling him.

Thirdly, when you are about to start the game, what do you think could possibly the results be?, either I win or my opponent wins or it is a draw, correct I said, so is there a fourth possibility and a fifth, no he said. So, if all the possible outcomes are known then you know for sure what happens ahead for each of the possibilities, "yes" he said, "kind of". So if you win you get two points, if your opponent wins you do not get a point and if it is a draw you get one point and each of this impacts your score and as of now you are at zero and there are 8 games to go. "Yes" he said "I am two games down", I stopped him right there, are you two games down or do you still have 8 games to win? What are you thinking about, "Joy of winning" or the "Fear of losing"? He smiled back; this time my little fella was prepared mentally. That day he won 3 of the 5 games he played and the next day he bettered the score to 4 out of 5 games. My little fella had matured one step ahead in life.

Building Sustainable
Financial Stability

The wealthy approach Work and Money differently than others. Wealthy do not work for the money to spend on things. They never spend their money on liabilities. They use their money to buy or create resources that generate money that also pays for those liabilities. This way they keep their money and still get the goodies.

Do they work sometimes? Yes, but only to create or build more money generating resources. They work to find ways to have their money make them more money. They work to find ways to have other people's money make them money. They leverage other people's time to make them money, like employees. They do not spend their time working for money and they do not spend their money on liabilities.

Others spend their time working for money. They spend their money on the stuff they want. They spend their time wondering how to "make some money". They have bills to pay and stuff to buy. So even if you are making the magic salary of RsX,XX,XX,XXX/- or even more or less in a year doesn't mean you are financially free, nor would you know if it is enough to become rich.

Above all regardless of how educated the wealthy are they are moneywise literate while the others are only financially literate. Let us look into a few important terms.

Cash flow

Simply put, cash flow is the flow of money in and out of my bank account. If more money flows out of my bank account than what comes in then I have a *negative* cash flow. I will then have to rectify it either by increasing the flow of money into my bank or reducing the flow of money

out of my bank. So, in which case I may choose to reduce my expenses to get back the balance or borrow money. Both these approaches are followed by those who continue to live in the "Struggle", making their compromises and making them "Struggle" even more intensely. In fact, the second approach of taking a loan generates long term guarantees of continued intense "Struggle" for a long time.

On the other hand if more money flows into my bank

than what goes out then I have a *positive* cash flow. This means that I have income more than my spending, i.e. I have "Disposable Income". Most people that I have seen living the "Struggle", can hardly trace where this disposable income got "Disposed" even before the month ended.

I have this great ex colleague from the army who recently got a promotion. He was doing very well in his career. With the increase in his salary his "Disposable income" increased. In the same week he upgraded his car and bought his first luxury watch. Now this is great, nothing wrong with it, except that the car loan and the personal loan he had taken to purchase these, thinking that he can pay off the loan from his increased salary was in fact making him live the "Struggle" even more intensely as he had higher monthly instalments to pay. There is nothing wrong in enjoying better quality of life; in fact you must strive to better your quality of life continuously. So you need to choose a path that will actually enable you to not just better your quality of life continuously but ENJOY it as well.

The key is in not in how much you earn but in how you spend. Expense patterns are important to understand, analyze and rationalize. To win the war of Sustained Financial Stability, let us understand a few conflict zones that you and I almost daily find ourselves in. Winning these is critical to create a Sustainable Financial Stability.

Personal Expense "Consumption Expense" & "Income Expense"

We spend on many things, food, clothes, movies, school fees, taxes, children's demands, holidays, healthcare and many more. All these expenses take money away from my hands, impacting my cash flow. If more money flows out of my hands than what comes in then I have a *negative* cash flow. But spending cannot be stopped we all need to survive and hence will always need to spend. Understanding how we spend is important so that I can spend to increase the flow of cash into my hands. Let me simplify by classifying expenses into two,

The first being the expense that I make for consumption; like groceries, electricity and maintenance for the house that I stay in, children's education, fine dining, and so on. These expenses are characterized by consumption i.e. we use it up for our day to day living. Let me term this as "Consumption Expense".

The other expense being the expense that I make, that increase the flow of cash into my hands; like buying a government bond that pays me interest free return, or the money I spent in buying real estate, or a Fixed Deposit that earns me an interest or the money I paid to buy the franchise of a popular fast food brand which I will use to start a business and earn profits. These are expenses that result in increasing my cash flow. Let me term this as "Income Expense".

So the monthly installment that I pay to the company that I took my housing loan from for the house that I am living in will be classified as a "Consumption Expense". On the other hand if I am not living in the house and earning a rent from the house then the monthly installment that I pay to the company that I took my housing loan from will be classified as "Income Expense". Similarly, for the loan EMI for the car that has been leased out, Expense made to buy assets like gold, that has the potential to appreciate or depreciate in value over a period of time are important expenses. They can add to my future cash flow, although they do not give me a monthly increase in cash flow I classify them as "Income Expense". These expenses once made need to be monitored regularly for its current value to ensure that it delivers returns greater than the current inflation.

We incur both these expenses. The interesting part is that it is possible to shift my spending pattern from "Consumption Expense" to "Income Expense". Well not entirely, but at least to the extent to start increasing the flow of cash into my hands.

Assets and Liabilities

Assets can be simply understood as resources that you have or acquire that generate income and / or appreciate in value which creates a promise for future cash flow. It brings money in my hand.

So, a Second home is an asset because I earn rent on it and enjoy tax benefits that reduce my Tax liability. The rent adds to the cash flow and the tax benefits reduce the cash flow away from my hand.

Liabilities can be simply understood as resources that you have or you acquire that make you spend your money that never comes back to you, that does not appreciate in value and / or even may depreciates in value. It takes money out of my hands.

So the expensive car that I drive around in is a liability as it depreciates in value every year and makes me spend on fuel, maintenance and the salary of my driver. If the money I spend does not come back to me, it is a liability.

So an "Asset" increases my cash flow and to make it happen, I make "Income Expense". "Liabilities" reduce my cash flow; I make a "Consumption Expense" to make it happen.

Risk and Opportunity

Ever since I was a child, I remember my parents telling me what was risky and what was not. How crossing the road when the pedestrian signal is red was risky and how we should use the zebra crossing otherwise there could be an accident and I could get hurt. Why I should be very careful when I am repairing any electrical appliances at home, or am in the kitchen near the gas stove. How by not studying I was running a risk of failing. As I grew up they told me how by not saving for the future I am risking my future, how the others will have a secure future and I will not. You know, they were not wrong at all.

We understand Risk as an uncertainty that could have an adverse effect leading to loss, harm or damage. The key words are "uncertainty" and "could have". So it is a probability of occurring that we need to deal with. The one thing that I learnt about risk was that it was there to stay. No matter how careful I was while I crossed the road, I could still land up in trouble if the motorist decided to break the signal. We see that kind of situation very often. The fact remains that every day we need to cook food on the gas / electric stove, and that you cannot live without

Risk is a permanent factor, you cannot wish it away, and all that you can do is to minimize the impact of or cater to contingency. You cannot avoid risk you need to manage it.

electricity. It is true that electricity is so powerful that it can roast you or power your air conditioner that cools you. In other words, it has to be managed. This is a reality, Risk is a permanent factor, you cannot wish it away, and all that you can do is to minimize the impact of or cater to contingency. You cannot avoid risk you need to manage it.

Opportunity is an event or a situation that can possibly happen, and if it does happen, we believe that it will bring benefits and / or rewards to us, tangible or non-tangible. In Opportunities, we see potential of gain that will benefit us or prevent us from losing. Opportunities, bring with them the "if" and "but", these are associated with risks. Risks associated with opportunities should be managed. If we look to avoid Risk, we will certainly avoid Opportunities.

THE CONFLICT ZONES
in the WAR to attain
Sustainable Financial Stability

The first conflict zone: Need and Want

A *NEED* is something you *have* to have, something you can't do without. A good example is food. If you don't eat, you won't survive for long. You can go hungry for a few days but eventually you have to eat food to survive. This is a real or a physical NEED. NEED, can be Psychological as well, like the NEED for Security. Feeling secured is more Psychological than real, but is still a NEED.

A *WANT* is something you *would like* to have. It is not absolutely necessary, but it would be a good thing to have. A good example is a mobile phone. The *need* is communication, the *want*, could be the latest phone launched.

For example; you *need* to eat protein, vitamins, and minerals. How you get them is up to you. You can eat meat, nuts, or soy products to get protein. You can get fruits and vegetables to get vitamins and minerals. You can eat yogurt or cheese to get other vitamins and minerals. So I NEED to eat protein, vitamins, and minerals and I WANT to eat meat and fruits.

The challenge is to understand clearly what a Need is and what is a Want and to have the wisdom and courage to clearly differentiate between the two and act accordingly. Needs are limited once satisfied, we attain psychological balance and feel satisfied, but WANT is the naughty one to watch for. When you satisfy one want the next one pops up.

"I NEED to keep in touch with my office; I NEED a Phone, I WANT the latest Phone launched." The conflict in this zone is our ability to continuously rationalize and stick to the NEED and not give in to the WANT. This is a psychological battle that is fought every day. So, *I NEED to keep in touch with my office; I NEED a Phone, I NEED access to my emails so I need a phone that gives me email and internet access so my choices are ......*

NEED can also grow as well, my earlier NEED was to insure my family for Rs 2,000,000/-, which I think should be adequate, now with the new baby in the house, we NEED to increase the insurance cover to Rs 2,500,0000/-.

Winning in this Conflict Zone means that you must be able to differentiate between "NEED" & "WANT" and to have the courage to act decisively. This is simply said than done.

The second conflict zone: Expense monitoring and planning

Most of those who are living the "Struggle" would tell you that they do not realize where their money goes after it lands in the bank account. When I started my first sales job, in the early 90's, I earned close to Rs 15,000/- per month. The money would get credited in my account by the 2nd of the month, and life would suddenly be great. Now starts the expenses, the new shirt that I always wanted to buy, wining and dining out, the avoidable luxury travel and so on. By the 18th of the month I suddenly realized that I have a balance of Rs 3000/- left, all this given that I stayed with my parents. Then all hell broke loose and all the compromises were made, luckily for me I rarely borrowed money for daily expense, for others it was worse. Those who borrowed money and spent it on the spoils of life would see a huge chunk of their salaries get washed away as soon as their money was credited only wanting them to borrow more every time.

This is not unique to me; it is pandemic with those who live the "Struggle". The key again is not how much you earn but how you spend, the pattern is important. As discussed earlier, spend we must, and the first step of improving the cash flow is to track the expense. What is not monitored is not measured and no improvement can be made. The challenge in this Battle Zone is to track expense consistently, month on month, year on year. This requires discipline that we all desire but very few of us acquire. The immediate benefits of tracking are that there is a self-monitoring that happens automatically and the result of this is visible almost immediately.

Track your expenses for a few months and you would see patterns emerge. Make a note of the payments that you can foresee like and insurance premium, utilities etc.

Winning in this Conflict Zone will need discipline in tracking expense.

The third conflict zone: Spending on consumption versus Spending money to earn more money

This is conflict is similar to driving in thick fog on a hill track. You really need to be sure which turn you need to take that will take you to your destination. If you keep taking the wrong turns then you will not only not reach your destination but also eventually run out of fuel and be stuck in the wilderness. Here what you need to be sure about is; are you spending your money on resources that bring money to you or are you spending your money on resources that take money away from your hand. Remember, Asset put money in my hand and create a positive cash flow and I need to do an Income Expense to buy asset. Liabilities take money out of my hands and create a negative cash flow and I need to do a "Consumption Expense" to buy Liabilities.

Frankly, who would really want to buy liabilities? No one would want to buy Liabilities, not knowingly to say the least. Still we have people buying Liabilities believing they are assets.

I always hated the deductions that show up on our pay slip every month, I am sure I am not the only one feeling so. The government through our employers forces us to make a few expenses that we are really not very happy about. Like for example, the employee provident fund (EPF). Most of us would classify it as a liability; it takes money away from my pocket and impacts my cash flow. I agree that it does. The best way to understand the difference between an Asset and a liability is to check what is the nature of the expense I am making, is this expense going to increase my cash flow? If yes then it is an "Income Expense" then it is an asset, else a liability.

So, EPF gave us a yearly rate of return of 8.5% last year which is more than the inflation which is around 4% the same year. This expense I am making is earning me income more than inflation. Also, if the account is more than 5 years old there will be no tax deducted when I close this account and withdraw my money, (if I want to) the government has no share in it. So this expense clearly brings in more money to my hands so I am making an "Income Expense" so I am buying an Asset. So, although, it is an expense and it takes money from my hand today is ensures cash flows for the future (time definite future in this case).

Winning in this Conflict Zone will need you to evaluate what are assets and liabilities and spend more on buying assets. The psychological battle front, spending on things on immediate gratification, "Consumption Expense" will need to be rationalized. This is easier said than done.

The fourth conflict zone: Risk and Opportunity

This conflict zone is a completely in our heads. Our reaction depends on our appetite for risk as well, not that this appetite cannot be developed. We understand Risk as an uncertainty that could have an adverse effect leading to loss, harm or damage. Now since Risk is a reality and that it is present now, creates a psychological imbalance / disturbance in our minds. This imbalance creates a threat of a loss which triggers our self-defense mechanism and we react to protect ourselves from this loss or threat. Let's understand this through an example.

For those of us who have tried their hands on swimming, would well be aware of what emotions we go through when we are face to face with the pool for the first time. I remember mine; it was an Olympic size pool that looked as big as the Arabian Sea to start with. The dream in my heart was to learn swimming and someday float in the water, sipping pineapple juice or may be a Margarita while I made my multimillion dollar deals. Well dreams are important so I dreamt. At the start it did not seem like that. With great strength I made it to the shallow part of the pool. I knew I cannot swim, so the risk of drowning was real. Even as a swimmer, I can drown. Strangely, the newspapers were carrying more news of accidents involving water I noticed in those days that I was learning to swim, more boat accident, drowning etc occurred, or was it that those were getting highlighted by my brain more than the usual? But one thing was sure I was afraid and the imbalance was created.

Then starts the "Coming to terms with" phase, standing on the edge of the shallow side of the pool, I started to rationalize; I am 5.7 ft the water is only 4 ft my head will be above the water and I will not go to the deep and hold the side bars so I will not drown, Also, I will wear a float, so I will be safe. Finally, with great courage, I jumped into the water, almost drowned and regained my balance. Once this happened, I got the feel that I can manage. Now, though the risk was there I learnt to handle it. I was happy at my achievement. And my calm (equilibrium) was restored, only to be shaken a week later, when my coach told me to move to the Deep side of the pool. The same challenge was relived.

Let's take another example, for most of us who live the "Struggle",

I need to have a house of my own in a good locality. To buy my dream home I need to take a housing loan, but the interest rates are high. I am hesitant to take a huge housing loan. *The dream of buying the house is driving me to take a risk of paying out a fixed EMI every month for the next 20 years.* Well I need to buy the house as I am going to get married and have kids someday; my current home is very small.

Then starts the rationalization; let me check with the housing loan company what would be my eligibility and what is the EMI going to be? On hearing from them, even if the EMI is on the higher side, but seems like a possibility, I start deciding how I will reduce my expense here and there so that I can pay off the EMI and of course there will be an increment next year and besides I am getting a Tax benefit on my housing loan. My dream house is now a possibility.

Then there are the "If" & "But". What if I lose my job? How will I pay the EMI? What if I repay part loan with my bonus money?

The Key to this is that our dreams are important to us and we need to make it happen, risks will always be there, which we need to rationalize and decide the way forward.

Winning in this Conflict Zone will need you to rationalize and analyze a Risk and the physiological imbalance that it creates in your mind. Your Dreams, Desires or Fears will push you on and want you to manage the Risk. To be successful in this Conflict Zone, you will also need to avoid discounting the Risk and fight the temptation of taking the Risk for granted.

Spending Habit

Your Spending habit is one of the key deciders of you not only getting Rich but also, Staying Rich. Firstly let us understand that Spending is important. We spend for essentials, we spend for pleasure, we spend in crises no matter what you cannot stop spending. In fact, I encourage spending, the catch is that we must spend more in resources that put money in my hand and not take money away from my hand.

Get hold of your expense details. What did you spend on? How much did you spend on? Classify them into "Consumption Expense" and "Income Expense". The first time I did this I suddenly discovered a lot about my spending habits. It was a little difficult for me to accept that I actually did some of these expenses. The moment something gets monitored it comes under control and is rationalized. That is good, an unintended outcome of this activity, but the idea was not to lower my standard of living, but on the contrary it is to increase my standard of living.

I kept tracking my spending regularly for the next 3 months, from the smallest to the biggest expense. With adequate data with me I decided to see what my numbers tell me. The beauty of data is that it tells the truth the way it is, it does not have 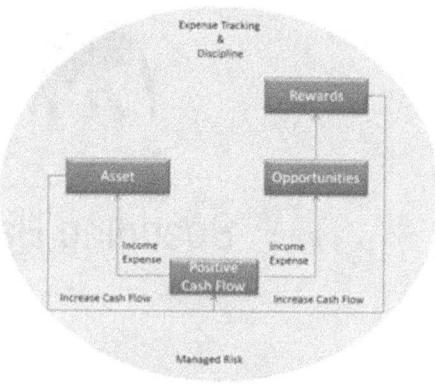 perceptions and it does not justify or defend anything, does not hide anything, it simply tells you the truth and so did my data that I had collected on spending. "Consumption Expenses" accounted for 92% of my total quarterly spending while "Income Expense" accounted for a mere 8 %. Shocked that I was, I was staring at a reality of my life that always existed but I just did not acknowledge. While my "Income Expense" was in most cases putting cash in my pocket as compared to the expense I was making, it was the "Consumption Expense" that was worrying me.

I looked through the "Consumption Expenses" with greater interest and this time I was looking for the details. While I maintain that I do not want to reduce my standard of living and rather increase it, cutting on expenses was not the option I was looking at. While I proactively eliminated what I thought was the completely unacceptable expenses, but they were really not very many and the impact was not significant, nevertheless it was important to be done. Now I turned my attention towards my increased "Consumptions Expense".

Of my 92% of "Consumption Expense" approximately 70% was spent on "Wants" and the balance 30% was spent on "Needs". While the "Needs" were essential and "Wants" were not, careful evaluation led me to understand that there was a lot more that I could do with my expense and gain more from the very same expense, in other words I need to "Sweat the Expense".

"Sweating the Expense"

"Sweating an Expense" refers to using the proceeds of the expense to the maximum. The Rich are actually good at it and the others are superb at it. A friend of mine had bought a very smart and expensive suit for his brother's wedding. He had a clear plan for the suit and the occasions that he would wear including office functions. He made the most of the expense. Not that he had only one suite. He actually had 3 suits, but what I liked was the fact that he had a clear plan for the each of his suits. I remember my suite I bought for my cousin's marriage, I never had a plan for its use later and as a result I actually never wore it. Eventually I had bought 4 suits for different reasons. Had I sweat my expense effectively; my expense would be better utilized and controlled as well.

Another great example of "Sweating an Expense" came from my subordinate; she was recently married and had moved into her new home that was pretty far from her office. This house was owned by the couple jointly. Office was an hour's drive during the office rush hours; sometimes it would take two hours depending on traffic. Late working hours and the heavy traffic was getting taxing on the couple. They decided to move in closer to her office which also reduced the drive time for her husband as well. They picked up a large apartment on rent that was very close to the office.

As she was narrating this over coffee, I could not help but get inquisitive and had a few questions for her. She said that she was happy to answer my questions. The discussion was very interesting, she had rented out her apartment that she owned and had moved in a rented apartment. So she tells me that the rent she receives offsets 90% of the rent she pays here. Her excitement was contagious as she narrated the details to me. My thoughts lingered on much after the conversation was over.

She had a component in her salary called the "House Rent Allowance". She was always taxed on this as she stayed with her parents who owned a nice house in a good locality. After all owning a home is a very emotional matter. This was an expense she was incurring, by moving out on rent, she would now get the benefit of the tax exemptions on HRA, besides the rental income, besides the tax benefit on the housing loan she has taken and also she will get the exemption on the maintenance on the house she has given on rent. What was earlier an expense she was now generating a positive cash flow on this account.

Operation "Positive Cash Flow"

The level of your Prosperity should be measured by the length of time that you could maintain your current standard of living without you having to earn anymore. In other words, if you had to stop working right now, how long could you keep up your current standard of living and continue to meet your current and the foreseeable expenses. There is no standard target number of months that you need to do to claim that you are now Rich and are prospering, so you need to set the target for yourself. I set my target as **"generating ancillary fixed income and / or incremental income twice my monthly liability"**.

The challenge is not just huge, but a little complex too. Every year the buying power of the currency reduces due to inflation, time value of money and factors beyond the control of an individual. If the purchasing power reduces, then I need to generate more money every year to enjoy the same standard of living I enjoy today. So I need to continuously have a positive cash flow even if I decide to stop working today, given that the expenses will only rise. This is possible when I build resources that incrementally increase the flow of cash in my hands. To achieve this, I need to put every rupee I earn to earn more, i.e. make more "Income Expense" and control "consumption Expense". We need to think in terms of a Defensive Strategy and an Offensive Strategy, with both being important.

Strengthening Defenses

Offence is the best form of defense, we all know this. To get on the offensive we first need to build strong defenses. It is only when we and our dear ones and their futures are secured that we can look to get offensive and get Prosperous. To win and continue winning Operation "Positive Cash Flow", we first need to minimize or eliminate the threats to my flow of cash. We need to identify the threats that can cause a negative cash flow. I call these defenses because in the event of a threat playing out you will be forced to defend against the threat that will result in your income money getting diverted to "Consumption Expense" leaving you with a negative cash flow situation. Worst case, if you have to take loans to meet your "Consumption Expense" your future cash out flow is assured and including the interest component, the out flow is significantly greater than the loan taken. So if I have not insured my family adequately, in case of a medical emergency, I will have to pay for it from my income. This is a "Consumption Expense". To meet my medical expense, if I take a loan then I add the interest payout to my cash out flow for the tenure of my loan. This is not a desirable situation.

Foreseeable threats are the easiest ones to deal with. Cash out flow in the form of Taxes are amongst biggest recurring expenses that impacts my Cash flow. The government was very active in my payslip and I knew it, except that I was not aware of the extent to which I was paying taxes. It was a direct result of my behavior of rarely flipping through my payslip in detail. I was paying almost a third of my salary to the Government. As a responsible citizen of this country I have always paid my taxes. I do not recommend that we default on our tax payments, but what I eventually realized in an effort to save taxes, I was, spending much more than what I would have paid taxes which had to change. Let me explain.

Taxes historically have been a very important income for the government. Rightly so, the government needs to pay for the roads, electricity and other civic amenities that any government is supposed to provide to the citizens. Tax structures vary from country to country and it is important that you know your countries tax structure. In India, the government calculates my tax payable after considering certain defined exemptions and then later gives me an opportunity to pay lesser taxes by offering me rebates. Good as it sounds, but this could be a honey trap. To save on the Tax payable, I need to show investments in certain predefined instruments, like insurance, housing loan, investment in government bonds etc. when I make investments within the limit mentioned, I save certain amount in of my tax liability. This is good and in certain cases it is great. Evaluating it from a cash flow perspective, I actually changed my mindset towards investments.

Let's take the example of Insurance. To save taxes, I bought policies giving me insurance cover and money back. I was happy when I bought them as I would get money in return at regular intervals. The shocker was when I started evaluating it, I had considerably less insurance cover and the return that these instruments gave me; in most cases it did not even beat the current inflation which was significantly high. Having investigated further I discovered that I had a range of options that I could exercise and fulfill my insurance needs, more importantly I learnt that insurance must not only be seen as an instrument to save taxes. These cases will differ country to country, it is important that you be fully aware about the tax structures in your country. Taking help of a qualified financial advisor or competent people is a good idea. They will be able to help you plan your finances well and also cater for future expenses and for contingencies as well.

Getting on the Offensive

The level of your Prosperity should be measured by the length of time that you can beat your expenses by your income month on month. So you could maintain your standard of living or improve it without any additional income from the business that you are currently involved in. In other words, if you had to stop working right now, how long could you keep up your current standard of living and continue to meet you current and the foreseeable expenses. The only way is to increase Income, given that I am not looking to reduce the current standard of living. However, the catch is that I can be involved in just one activity at a time; it could be business or employment and have only 24 hours a day. So how do I increase my cash flow without generating it myself?

The solution lies in the way we spend the money from our positive cash flow to develop more earning members. When you make additional money either through your bonus or in the stock market, you may be tempted to spend it on "Consumption expense", like latest phone, the branded shirt you always wanted to buy. If the expense is a "Need" then the expense has to be done, i.e. "Consumption Expense", but if it is a "Want" then it would be wiser to divert this money into "Income Expense" first. Use the opportunity to make an "Income Expense" build an additional earning member generate the additional cash flow and buy your Want.

So if you choose to invest this surplus in a, for example, in a fixed deposit it will bring in additional money for you. My neighbor is a young couple employed in the private sector. The couple had earned a total bonus of Rs3, 75,000/-. They bought a midsize car, they were happy and so were the children, but they hardly used the car, as they took the local train to office. They would give it on hire purchase when the family was not using the car. The money received, was used to pay for the maintenance and the driver salary, sometimes they had surplus generated as well. They had successfully added an earning member in their family.

Cycling and Recycling

Surplus generated from income from the earning members that you add should be recycled with the earning member. So the income that I generate from the fixed deposit I reinvest it in the Fixed Deposit and the cycle goes on. The neighbor couple mentioned earlier should also be doing so, that will enable them to have more vehicles and larger revenue. As the revenue increases, you must pay yourself first from the surplus that you are generating, before you start allocating it back to the earning member.

Know When to Quit

Every earning member added needs to be constantly checked for relevance and the capacity to generate revenue. So if the inflation goes beyond the interest earned in a Fixed Deposit, then the ability of the member to generate money has diminished. We need to be aware when to move away. Know when to walk away from a loss, and don't let anxiety fool you into trying again.

Conclusion

The history of mankind is a saga of valor and grit that have defied the storms of time and adversities in a relentless pursuit of dreams and desires. History was made because we dare to dream and have been stubborn to achieve. Military history is also full of many heroics regard less of which side they fought from. In the military academy we have studied many battles and have learnt from it. Subsequently I continued reading a lot on campaigns fought across the globe especially the two World Wars. Of the many amazing battles, some have remained etched in my memory. One such battle was the Battle of Stalingrad and in particular the heroics of a particular solider Vasily Zaitsev.

Stalingrad was a city named after the Russian Leader, Joseph Stalin. Stalingrad was attacked ruthlessly by the advancing German Army. Russia was losing the war and Stalingrad was probably the last attempt to halt the advancing Germans. This Battle changed the course of the War. The battle was fought mostly by untrained and poorly armed men, women and in some cases children against a well-armed German army. One particular solider, Vasily Zaitsev, made a distinction for himself as a sniper in this Battle. His heroics boosted the Soviet soldiers' morale in their superhuman defense of Stalingrad. He became the picture of hope, success and their Spirit at a time when the Russians were down and were facing their toughest battle. During the Battle of Stalingrad, he eliminated 242 soldiers and officers, including 11 enemy snipers, but the rumors were that the real number may be much higher. His rifle the standard-issue Mosin-Nagant rifle is a national treasure today.

A simple farm boy, Vasily Zaitsev was born in the Ural Mountains and honed his skills hunting deer and wolf with his grandfather. Originally serving in the Soviet Navy as a clerk, but choose to volunteer and be sent to the front line at the start of the German invasion. Zaitsev was a special individual, his ability to dream, to believe in his dreams, being stubbornly positive despite all odds, stubbornness to achieve and flexibility in his approach made him achieve what he did and that made him special. There is a solider is us too. All of us who live through the "Struggle" are soldiers in our own right and we too have dreams that we chase daily. With belief in our dreams and in our own abilities, we can achieve our dreams, if we so choose to and stay doggedly focused on achieving it.